CARYL CHURCHILL

Caryl Churchill has written for the stage, television and radio. Her stage plays include *Owners* (Royal Court Theatre Upstairs, 1972); *Objections to Sex and Violence* (Royal Court, 1975); *Light Shining in Buckinghamshire* (Joint Stock on tour incl. Royal Court Upstairs, 1976); *Vinegar Tom* (Monstrous Regiment on tour, incl. Half Moon and ICA, 1976); *Traps* (Royal Court Upstairs, 1977); *Cloud Nine* (Joint Stock on tour incl. Royal Court, 1979, then Theatre de Lys, New York, 1981); *Three More Sleepless Nights* (Soho Poly and Royal Court Upstairs, 1980); *Top Girls* (Royal Court, then Public Theater, New York, 1982); *Fen* (Joint Stock on tour, incl. Almeida and Royal Court, then Public Theater, New York, 1983); *Softcops* (RSC at the Pit, 1984); *A Mouthful of Birds* with David Lan (Joint Stock on tour, incl. Royal Court, 1986); *Serious Money* (Royal Court and Wyndham's, London, then Public Theater, New York, 1987); *Icecream* (Royal Court, 1989); *Mad Forest* (Central School of Speech and Drama, then Royal Court, 1990); *Lives of the Great Poisoners* with Orlando Gough and Ian Spink (Second Stride on tour, incl. Riverside Studios, London, 1991); *The Skriker* (Royal National Theatre, 1994); *Thyestes* translated from Seneca (Royal Court Upstairs, 1994); *Hotel* with Orlando Gough and Ian Spink (Second Stride on tour, incl. The Place, London, 1997); *This is a Chair* (London International Festival of Theatre at the Royal Court, 1997); *Blue Heart* (Joint Stock on tour, incl. Royal Court, 1997); *Far Away* (Royal Court Upstairs, 2000, and Albery, London, 2001, then New York Theatre Workshop, 2002); *A Number* (Royal Court Downstairs, 2002, then New York Theatre Workshop, 2004); *A Dream Play* after Strindberg (Royal National Theatre, 2005); *Drunk Enough to Say I Love You?* (Royal Court Downstairs, 2006, then Public Theater, New York, 2008); *Bliss* translated from Olivier Choinière (Royal Court Upstairs, 2008); *Seven Jewish Children – a play for Gaza* (Royal Court, 2009).

Other works by Caryl Churchill, published by Nick Hern Books

Light Shining in Buckinghamshire
Traps
Cloud Nine
Icecream
Mad Forest
The Skriker
Thyestes (translated from Seneca)
Hotel
This is a Chair
Blue Heart
A Number
A Dream Play (translated from Strindberg)
Drunk Enough to Say I Love You?
Bliss (translated from Olivier Choinière)
Seven Jewish Children

Collections

Plays: Three
   A Mouthful of Birds (with David Lan)
   Icecream
   Mad Forest
   Lives of the Great Poisoners (with Orlando Gough and Ian Spink)
   The Skriker
   Thyestes

Plays: Four
   Hotel
   This is a Chair
   Blue Heart
   Far Away
   A Number
   A Dream Play (translated from Strindberg)
   Drunk Enough to Say I Love You?

Shorts
   Lovesick
   Abortive
   Not Not Not Not Not Enough Oxygen
   Schreber's Nervous Illness
   The Hospital at the Time of the Revolution
   The Judge's Wife
   The After-Dinner Joke
   Seagulls
   Three More Sleepless Nights
   Hot Fudge

CARYL CHURCHILL

A Number

London

NICK HERN BOOKS

www.nickhernbooks.co.uk

A Nick Hern Book

A Number first published in Great Britain as a paperback original
in 2002 by Nick Hern Books Limited, 14 Larden Road,
London W3 7ST

Reprinted 2003, 2004, 2008, 2009, 2010

A Number copyright © 2002 Caryl Churchill Ltd

Caryl Churchill has asserted her right to be identified as the author
of this work

Typeset by Country Setting, Kingsdown, Kent CT14 8ES
Printed in Great Britain by CPI Antony Rowe, Chippenham,
Wiltshire

A CIP catalogue record for this book is available from
the British Library

ISBN   978 1 85459 743 4

A Number was first performed by Michael Gambon
and Daniel Craig at the Royal Court Theatre, London,
on 23 September 2002. The play was directed by
Stephen Daldry and designed by Ian MacNeil. Lighting
was designed by Rick Fisher and Ian Dickinson was the
sound designer.

US premiere by New York Theatre Workshop.

Characters

SALTER, *a man in his early sixties*

BERNARD, *his son, forty*

BERNARD, *his son, thirty-five*

MICHAEL BLACK, *his son, thirty-five*

The play is for two actors. One plays Salter, the other his sons.

The scene is the same throughout, it's where Salter lives.

1

SALTER, *a man in his early sixties and his son* BERNARD (B2), *thirty-five.*

B2   A number

SALTER   you mean

B2   a number of them, of us, a considerable

SALTER   say

B2   ten, twenty

SALTER   didn't you ask?

B2   I got the impression

SALTER   why didn't you ask?

B2   I didn't think of asking.

SALTER   I can't think why not, it seems to me it would be the first thing you'd want to know, how far has this thing gone, how many of these things are there?

B2   Good, so if it ever happens to you

SALTER   no you're right

B2   no it was stupid, it was shock, I'd known for a week before I went to the hospital but it was still

SALTER   it is, I am, the shocking thing is that
                there *are* these, not how many but at all

B2   even one

SALTER   exactly, even one, a twin would be a
                shock

B2   a twin would be a surprise but a number

SALTER   a number any number is a shock.

B2   You said things, these things

SALTER   I said?

B2   you called them things. I think we'll find
                they're people.

SALTER   Yes of course they are, they are of
                course.

B2   Because I'm one.

SALTER   No.

B2   Yes. Why not? Yes.

SALTER   Because they're copies

B2   copies? they're not

SALTER   copies of you which some mad scientist
                has illegally

B2   how do you know that?

SALTER   I don't but

B2   what if someone else is the one, the first
                one, the real one and I'm

SALTER   no because

B2   not that I'm *not* real which is why I'm
              saying they're not things, don't call them

SALTER   just wait, because I'm your father.

B2   You know that?

SALTER   Of course.

B2   It was all a normal, everything, birth

SALTER   you think I wouldn't know if I wasn't
              your father?

B2   Yes of course I was just for a moment
              there, but they are all still people like
              twins are all, quins are all

SALTER   yes I'm sorry

B2   we just happen to have identical be
              identical identical genetic

SALTER   sorry I said things, I didn't mean
              anything by that, it just

B2   no forget it, it's nothing, it's

SALTER   because of course for me you're the

B2   yes I know what you meant, I just,
              because of course I want them to be
              things, I do think they're things, I don't
              think they're, of course I *do* think they're
              them just as much as I'm me but I. I
              don't know what I think, I feel terrible.

SALTER   I wonder if we can sue.

B2	Sue? who?
SALTER	Them, whoever did it. Who did you see?
B2	Just some young, I don't know, younger than me.
SALTER	So who did it?
B2	He's dead, he was some old and they've just found the records and they've traced
SALTER	so we sue the hospital.
B2	Maybe. Maybe we can.
SALTER	Because they've taken your cells
B2	but when how did they?
SALTER	when you were born maybe or later you broke your leg when you were two you were in the hospital, some hairs or scrapings of your skin
B2	but they didn't damage
SALTER	but it's you, part of you, the value
B2	the value of those people
SALTER	yes
B2	and what is the value of
SALTER	there you are, who knows, priceless, and they belong
B2	no
SALTER	they belong to you, they should belong to you, they're made from your

B2   they should

SALTER   they've been stolen from you and you
               should get your rights

B2   but is it

SALTER   what? is it money? is it something you
               can put a figure on? put a figure on it.

B2   This is purely

SALTER   yes

B2   suppose each person was worth ten
               thousand pounds

SALTER   a hundred

B2   a hundred thousand?

SALTER   they've taken a person away from you

B2   times the number of people

SALTER   which we don't know

B2   but a number a fairly large say anyway
               ten

SALTER   a million is the least you should take, I
               think it's more like half a million each
               person because what they've done
               they've damaged your uniqueness,
               weakened your identity, so we're looking
               at five million for a start.

B2   Maybe.

SALTER   Yes, because how dare they?

B2	We'd need to be able to prove
SALTER	we prove you're genetically my son genetically and then
B2	because there's no doubt
SALTER	no doubt at all. I suppose you didn't see one?
B2	One what? of them?
SALTER	of these people
B2	no I think they'd keep us apart wouldn't they so we don't spoil like contaminate the crime scene so you don't tell each other I have nightmares oh come to think of it I have nightmares and he might have said no if he was asked in the first place
SALTER	because they need to find out
B2	yes how much we're the same, not just how tall we are or do we get asthma but what do you call your dog, why did you leave your wife you don't even know the answer to these questions.
SALTER	So you didn't suddenly suddenly see
B2	what suddenly see myself coming round the corner
SALTER	because that could be
B2	like seeing yourself on the camera in a shop or you hear yourself on the

	answering machine and you think god is that what I

SALTER   but more than that, it'd be it'd be

B2   don't they say you die if you meet yourself?

SALTER   walk round the corner and see yourself you could get a heart attack. Because if that's me over there who am I?

B2   Yes but it's not me over there

SALTER   no I know

B2   it's like having a twin that's all it's just

SALTER   I know what it is.

B2   I think I'd like to meet one. It's an adventure isn't it and you're part of science. I wouldn't be frightened to meet any number.

SALTER   I don't know.

B2   They're all your sons.

SALTER   I don't want a number of sons, thank you, you're plenty, I'm fine.

B2   Maybe after they've found everything out they'll let us meet. They'll have a party for us, we can

SALTER   I'm not going to drink with those doctors. But maybe you're right you're right, take it in a positive spirit.

B2   There is a thing

SALTER   what's that?

B2   a thing that puzzles me a little

SALTER   what's that?

B2   I did get the impression and I know I
                may be wrong because maybe I was in
                shock but I got the impression there was
                this batch and we were all in it. I was in
                it.

SALTER   No because you're my son.

B2   No but we were all

SALTER   I explained already

B2   but I wasn't being quite open with you
                because I'm confused because it's a shock
                but I want to know what happened

SALTER   they stole

B2   no but what happened

SALTER   I don't

B2   because they said that none of us was
                the original.

SALTER   They said that?

B2   I think

SALTER   I think you're mistaken because you're
                confused

B2   you think

SALTER   you need to get back to them

B2   well I'll do that. But I think that's what
              they meant

SALTER   it's not what they meant

B2   ok. But that's my impression, that none
              of us is the original.

SALTER   Then who? do they know?

B2   they're not saying, they just say we were
              all

SALTER   they're not saying?

B2   so if I was your son the original would
              be your son too which is nonsense so

SALTER   does that follow?

B2   so please if you're not my father that's
              fine. If you couldn't have children or my
              mother, and you did in vitro or I don't
              know what you did I really think you
              should tell me.

SALTER   Yes, that's what it was.

B2   That's all right.

SALTER   Yes I know.

B2   Thank you for telling me.

SALTER   Yes.

B2   It's better to know.

SALTER   Yes.

B2   So don't be upset.

SALTER   No.

B2   You are though

SALTER   Well.

B2   I'm fine about it. I'm not quite sure
              what I'm fine about. There was some
              other person this original some baby or
              cluster or and there were a number a
              number of us made somehow and you
              were one of the people who acquired,
              something like that.

SALTER   It wasn't

B2   don't worry

SALTER   because the thing is you see that isn't
              what happened. I am your father, it was
              by an artificial the forefront of science
              but I am genetically.

B2   That's great.

SALTER   Yes.

B2   So I know the truth and you're still my
              father and that's fine.

SALTER   Yes.

B2   So what about this original? I don't quite
              I don't

SALTER   There was someone.

B2   There was what kind of someone?

SALTER   There was a son.

B2   A son of yours?

SALTER   Yes.

B2   So when was that?

SALTER   That was some time earlier.

B2   Some time before I was born there was

SALTER   another son, yes, a first

B2   who what, who died

SALTER   who died, yes

B2   and you wanted to replace him

SALTER   I wanted

B2   instead of just having another child you wanted

SALTER   because your mother was dead too

B2   but she died when I was born, I thought she

SALTER   well I'm telling you what happened.

B2   So what happened?

SALTER   So they'd been killed in a carcrash and

B2   my mother and this

SALTER   carcrash

B2   when was this? how old was the child, was he

SALTER   four, he was four

B2   and you wanted him back

SALTER   yes

B2   so I'm just him over again.

SALTER   No but you are you because that's who
            you are but I wanted one just the same
            because that seemed to me the most
            perfect

B2   but another child might have been better

SALTER   no I wanted the same

B2   but I'm not him

SALTER   no but you're just the way I wanted

B2   but I could have been a different person
            not like him I

SALTER   how could you? if I'd had a different
            child that wouldn't be you, would it.
            You're this one.

B2   I'm just a copy. I'm not the real one.

SALTER   You're the only one.

B2   What do you mean only, there's all the
            others, there's

SALTER   but I didn't know that, that wasn't part
            of the deal. They were meant to make
            one of you not a whole number, they
            stole that, we'll deal with, it's something
            for lawyers. But you're what I wanted,
            you're the one.

B2   Did you give me the same name as him?

SALTER   Does it make it worse?

B2   Probably.

2

SALTER *and his other son* BERNARD (B1), *forty.*

SALTER   So they stole – don't look at me – they
          stole your genetic material and

B1   no

SALTER   they're the ones you want to

B1   no

SALTER   because what ten twenty twenty copies of
          you walking round the streets

B1   no

SALTER   which was nothing to do with me
          whatsoever and I think you and I should
          be united on this.

B1   Let me look at you.

SALTER   You've been looking at me all the

B1   let me look at you.

SALTER   Bit older.

B1   No because your father's not young
          when you're small is he, he's not any
          age, he's more a power. He's a dark dark
          power which is why my heart, people
          pay trainers to get it up to this speed,
          but is it because my body recognises or

because I'm told? because if I'd seen you
in the street I don't think I'd've stopped
and shouted Daddy. But you'd've known
me wouldn't you. Unless you thought I
was one of the others.

SALTER   It's a long time.

B1   Can we talk about what you did?

SALTER   Yes of course. I'm not sure where what

B1   about you sent me away and had this
other one made from some bit of my
body some

SALTER   it didn't hurt you

B1   what bit

SALTER   I don't know what

B1   not a limb, they clearly didn't take a
limb like a starfish and grow

SALTER   a speck

B1   or half of me chopped through like a
worm and grow the other

SALTER   a scraping cells a speck a speck

B1   a speck yes because we're talking that
microscope world of giant blobs and
globs

SALTER   that's all

B1   and they take this painless scrape this
specky little cells of me and kept that
and you threw the rest of me away

SALTER   no

B1   and had a new one made

SALTER   no

B1   yes

SALTER   yes

B1   yes

SALTER   yes of course, you know I did, I'm not
             attempting to deny, I thought it was the
             best thing to do, it seemed a brilliant it
             was the only

B1   brilliant?

SALTER   it seemed

B1   to get rid

SALTER   it wasn't perfect. It was the best I could
             do, I wasn't very I was I was always and
             it's a blur to be honest but it was I
             promise you the best

B1   and this copy they grew of me, that
             worked out all right?

SALTER   There were failures of course, inevitable

B1   dead ones

SALTER   in the test tubes the dishes, I was told
             they didn't all

B1   but they finally got a satisfactory a
             bouncing

SALTER   yes but they lied to me because they
          didn't tell me

B1   in a cradle

SALTER   all those others, they stole

B1   and he looked just like me did he
          indistinguishable from

SALTER   yes

B1   so it worked out very well. And this son
          lives and breathes?

SALTER   yes

B1   talks and fucks? eats and walks? swims
          and dreams and exists somewhere right
          now yes does he? exist now?

SALTER   yes

B1   still exists

SALTER   yes of course

B1   happily?

SALTER   well mostly you could say

B1   as happily as most people?

SALTER   yes I think

B1   because most people are happy I read in
          the paper. Did it cost a lot of money?

SALTER   the procedure? to get?

B1   the baby

SALTER   yes.

B1   Were we rich?

SALTER   Not rich.

B1   No, I don't remember anything rich. A
             lot of dust under the bed those heaps of
             fluff you get don't you if you look if you
             go under there and lie in it.

SALTER   No, we weren't. But I managed. I was
             spending less.

B1   You made an effort.

SALTER   I did and for that money you'd think I'd
             get exclusive

B1   they ripped you off

SALTER   because one one was the deal and they

B1   what do you expect?

SALTER   from you too they it's you they, just so
             they can do some scientific some
             research some do you get asthma do you
             have a dog what do you call it do you

B1   Who did you think it was at the door?
             did you think it was one of the others or
             your son or

SALTER   I don't know the others

B1   you know your son

SALTER   I know

B1   your son the new

SALTER   yes of course

B1   you know him

SALTER   yes I wouldn't think he was you, no.

B1   You wouldn't think it was him having a bad day.

SALTER   You look very well.

B1   But it could have been one of the others?

SALTER   Yes because that's what I was thinking about, how could the doctors, I think there's money to be made out of this.

B1   I've not been lucky with dogs. I had this black and tan bitch wouldn't do what it's told, useless. Before that I had a lurcher they need too much running about. Then a friend of mine went inside could I look after, battle from day one with that dog, rottweiler pit bull I had to throw a chair, you could hit it with a belt it kept coming back. I'd keep it shut up in the other room and it barks so you have to hit it, I was glad when it bit a girl went to pat it and straight off to the vet, get rid of this one it's a bastard. My friend wasn't pleased but he shouldn't have gone in the postoffice.

SALTER   No that's right. I've never wanted a dog.

B1   Don't patronise me

SALTER   I'm not I'm not

B1   you don't know what you're doing

SALTER   I just

B1   because you go in a pub someone throws
            his beer in your face you're supposed to
            say sorry, he only had three stitches I'm
            a very restrained person. Because this
            minute we sit here there's somebody a lot
            of them but think of one on the electric
            bedsprings or water poured down his
            throat and jump on his stomach. There's
            a lot of wicked people. So that's why.
            And you see them all around you. You
            go down the street and you see their
            faces and you think you don't fool me
            I know what you're capable of. So don't
            start anything.

SALTER   I think what we need is a good solicitor.

B1   What I like about a dog it stops people
            getting after you, they're not going to
            come round in the night. But they make
            the place stink because I might want to
            stay out a few days and when I get back
            I might want to stay in a few days and
            a dog can become a tyrant to you.

            Silence.

            Hello daddy daddy daddy, daddy hello.

SALTER   Nobody regrets more than me the
            completely unforeseen unforeseeable
            which isn't my fault and does make it
            more upsetting but what I did did seem
            at the time the only and also it's a
            tribute, I could have had a different one,
            a new child altogether that's what most

people but I wanted you again because I thought you were the best.

B1   It wasn't me again.

SALTER   No but the same basic the same raw materials because they were perfect. You were the most beautiful baby everyone said. As a child too you were very pretty, very pretty child.

B1   You know when I used to be shouting.

SALTER   No.

B1   When I was there in the dark. I'd be shouting.

SALTER   No.

B1   Yes, I'd be shouting dad dad

SALTER   Was this some time you had a bad dream or?

B1   shouting on and on

SALTER   I don't think I

B1   shouting and shouting

SALTER   no

B1   and you never came, nobody ever came

SALTER   so was this after your mum

B1   after my mum was dead this was after

SALTER   because you were very little when she

B1   yes because I can only remember

SALTER   you were maybe two when she

B1   and I remember her sitting there, she
              was there

SALTER   you remember so early?

B1   she'd be there but she wouldn't help stop
              anything

SALTER   I'm surprised

B1   so when I was shouting what I want to
              know

SALTER   but when was this

B1   I want to know if you could hear me or
              not because I never knew were you
              hearing me and not coming or could you
              not hear me and if I shouted loud
              enough you'd come

SALTER   I can't have heard you, no

B1   or maybe there was no one there at all
              and you'd gone out so no matter how
              hard I shouted there was no one there

SALTER   no that wouldn't have

B1   so then I'd stop shouting but it was
              worse

SALTER   because I hardly ever

B1   and I didn't dare get out of bed to go
              and see

SALTER   I don't think this can have

B1   because if there was nobody there that
              would be terrifying and if you were there

	that might be worse but it's something I wonder
SALTER	no
B1	could you hear me shouting?
SALTER	no I don't
B1	no
SALTER	no I don't think this happened in quite the
B1	what?
SALTER	because I'd
B1	again and again and again, every night I'd be
SALTER	no
B1	so you didn't hear?
SALTER	no but you can't have
B1	yes I was shouting, are you telling me you didn't
SALTER	no of course I didn't
B1	you didn't
SALTER	no
B1	you weren't sitting there listening to me shouting
SALTER	no
B1	you weren't out

SALTER	no
B1	so I needed to shout louder.
SALTER	Of course sometimes everyone who's had children will tell you sometimes you put them to bed and they want another story and you say goodnight now and go away and they call out once or twice and you say no go to sleep now and they might call out again and they go to sleep.
B1	The other one. Your son. My brother is he? my little twin.
SALTER	Yes.
B1	Has he got a child?
SALTER	No.
B1	Because if he had I'd kill it.
SALTER	No, he hasn't got one.
B1	So when you opened the door you didn't recognise me.
SALTER	No because
B1	Do you recognise me now?
SALTER	I know it's you.
B1	No but look at me.
SALTER	I have. I am.
B1	No, look in my eyes. No, keep looking. Look.

3

SALTER *and* BERNARD (B2).

B2   Not like me at all

SALTER   not like

B2   well like like but not identical not

SALTER   not identical no not

B2   because what struck me was how different

SALTER   yes I was struck

B2   you couldn't mistake

SALTER   no no not at all I knew at once it wasn't

B2   though of course he is older if I was older

SALTER   but even then you wouldn't

B2   I wouldn't be identical

SALTER   no no not at all no, you're a different

B2   just a bit like

SALTER   well bound to be a bit

B2   because for a start I'm not frightening.

SALTER   So what did he want did he

B2   no nothing really, not frightening not

SALTER   he didn't hit you?

B2   hit? god no, hit me? do you think?

SALTER   well he

B2   he could have done yes, no he shouted

SALTER   shouted

B1   shouted and rambled really, rambled he's
              not entirely

SALTER   no, well

B2   so that's what, his childhood, his life, his
              childhood

SALTER   all kinds of

B2   has made him a nutter really is what I
              think I mean not a nutter but he's

SALTER   yes yes I'm not, yes he probably is.

B2   He says all kinds of wild

SALTER   yes

B2   so you don't know what to believe.

SALTER   And how did it end up, are you on
              friendly

B2   friendly no

SALTER   not

B2   no no we ended up

SALTER   yes

B2   we ended as I mean to go on with me
            running away, I was glad we were
            meeting in a public place, if I'd been at
            home you can't run away in your own
            home and if we'd been at his I wonder if
            he'd have let me go he might put me in
            a cupboard not really, anyway yes I got
            up and left and I kept thinking had he
            followed me.

SALTER   As you mean to go on as in not seeing
            him any more

B2   as in leaving the country.

SALTER   For what for a week or two a holiday, I
            don't

B2   leaving, going on yes I don't know, going
            away, I don't want to be here.

SALTER   But when you come back he'll still

B2   so maybe I won't

SALTER   but that's, not come back, no that's

B2   I don't know I don't know don't ask me
            I don't know. I'm going, I don't know. I
            don't want to be anywhere near him.

SALTER   You think he might try to hurt you?

B2   Why? why do you keep

SALTER   I don't know. Is it that?

B2   It's partly that, it's also it's horrible, I
            don't feel myself and there's the others

too, I don't want to see them I don't
want them

SALTER   I thought you did.

B2   I thought I did, I might, if I go away
by myself I might feel all right, I might
feel – you can understand that.

SALTER   Yes, yes I can.

B2   Because there's this person who's
identical to me

SALTER   he's not

B2   who's not identical, who's like

SALTER   not even very

B2   not very like but very something terrible
which is exactly the same genetic person

SALTER   not the same person

B2   and I don't like it.

SALTER   I know. I'm sorry.

B2   I know you're sorry I'm not

SALTER   I know

B2   I'm not trying to make you say sorry

SALTER   I know, I just am

B2   I know

SALTER   I just am sorry.

B2   He said some things.

SALTER   Yes.

B2   There's a lot of things I don't, could you tell me what happened to my mother?

SALTER   She's dead.

B2   Yes.

SALTER   I told you she was dead.

B2   Yes but she didn't die when I was born and she didn't die with the first child in a carcrash because the first child's not dead he's walking round the streets at night giving me nightmares. Unless she did die in a carcrash?

SALTER   No.

B2   No.

SALTER   Your mother, the thing a thing about your mother was that she wasn't very happy, she wasn't a very happy person at all, I don't mean there were sometimes days she wasn't happy or I did things that made her not happy I did of course, she was always not happy, often cheerful and

B2   she killed herself. How did she do that?

SALTER   She did it under a train under a tube train, she was one of those people when they say there has been a person under a train and the trains are delayed she was a person under a train.

B2   Were you with her?

SALTER   With her on the platform no, I was still
            with her more or less but not with her
            then no I was having a drink I think.

B2   And the boy?

SALTER   Do you know I don't remember where
            the boy was. I think he was at a friend's
            house, we had friends.

B2   And he was how old four?

SALTER   no no he was four later when I he was
            walking, about two just starting to talk

B2   he was four when you sent him

SALTER   that's right when his mother died he was
            two.

B2   So this was let me be clear this was
            before this was some years before I was
            born she died before

SALTER   yes

B2   so she was already always

SALTER   yes she was

B2   just so I'm clear. And then you and the
            boy you and your son

SALTER   we went on we just

B2   lived alone together

SALTER   yes

B2	you were bringing him up
SALTER	yes
B2	the best you could
SALTER	I
B2	until
SALTER	and my best wasn't very but I had my moments, don't think, I did cook meals now and then and read a story I'm sure I can remember a particularly boring and badly written little book about an elephant at sea. But I could have managed better.
B2	Yes he said something about it
SALTER	he said
B2	yes
SALTER	yes of course he did yes. I know I could have managed better because I did with you because I stopped, shut myself away, gave it all up came off it all while I waited for you and I think we may even have had that same book, maybe it's you I remember reading it to, do you remember it at all? it had an elephant in red trousers.
B2	No I don't think
SALTER	no it was terrible, we had far better books we had

B2   Maybe he shouldn't blame you, maybe it
            was a genetic, could you help drinking
            we don't know or drugs at the time
            philosophically as I understand it it
            wasn't viewed as not like now when our
            understanding's different and would a
            different person genetically different
            person not have been so been so
            vulnerable because there could always be
            some genetic addictive and then again
            someone with the same genetic exactly
            the same but at a different time a
            different cultural and of course all the
            personal all kinds of what happened in
            your own life your childhood or things
            all kind of because suppose you'd had a
            brother with identical an identical twin
            say but separated at birth so you had
            entirely different early you see what I'm
            saying would he have done the same
            things who can say he might have been
            a very loving father and in fact of course
            you have that in you to be that because
            you were to me so it's a combination of
            very complicated and that's who you
            were so probably I shouldn't blame you.

SALTER   I'd rather you blamed me. I blame
            myself.

B2   I'm not saying you weren't horrible.

SALTER   Couldn't I not have been?

B2   Apparently not.

SALTER   If I'd tried harder.

B2   But someone like you couldn't have tried harder. What does it mean? If you'd tried harder you'd have been different from what you were like and you weren't you were

SALTER   but then later I

B2   later yes

SALTER   I did try that's what I did I started again I

B2   that's what

SALTER   I was good I tried to be good I was good to you

B2   that's what you were like

SALTER   I was good

B2   but I can't you can't I can't give you credit for that if I don't give you blame for the other it's what you did it's what happened

SALTER   but it felt

B2   it felt

SALTER   it felt as if I tried I deliberately

B2   of course it felt

SALTER   well then

B2   it feels it always it feels doesn't it inside that's just how we feel what we are and

we don't know all these complicated we
can't know what we're it's too
complicated to disentangle all the causes
and we feel this is me I freely and of
course it's true who you are does freely
not forced by someone else but who you
are who you are itself forces or you'd be
someone else wouldn't you?

SALTER   I did some bad things. I deserve to
suffer. I did some better things. I'd like
recognition.

B2   That's how everyone feels, certainly.

SALTER   He still blames me.

B2   There's a difference then.

SALTER   You remind me of him.

B2   I remind myself of him. We both hate
you.

SALTER   I thought you

B2   I don't blame you it's not your fault but
what you've been like what you're like
I can't help it.

SALTER   Yes of course.

B2   Except what he feels as hate and what
I feel as hate are completely different
because what you did to him and what
you did to me are different things.

SALTER   I was nice to you.

B2   Yes you were.

SALTER   You don't have to go away. Not for long.

B2   It might make me feel better.

SALTER   I love you.

B2   That's something else you can't help.

SALTER   That's all right. That's all right.

B2   Also I'm afraid he'll kill me.

4

SALTER *and* BERNARD (B1).

SALTER   So what kind of a place was it? was it

B1   the place

SALTER   he was in a hotel was he or

B1   no

SALTER   I thought he was in a hotel. So where was he?

B1   what?

SALTER   I'm trying to get a picture.

B1   Does it matter?

SALTER   It won't bring him back no obviously but I'd like I'd like you can't help feeling curious you want to get at it and you're blocked in all directions, your son dies you want his body, you want to know where his body last was when he was alive, you can't help

B1   He had a room.

SALTER   In somebody's house, renting

B1   some small you know how the locals when you arrive, just a room not breakfast you'd go out for a coffee.

SALTER   So was it some pretty on a harbour front
           or

B1   no

SALTER   thinking of him on holiday

B1   in a street just a side

SALTER   but of course it wasn't a holiday he was
          hiding he thought he was hiding. Did
          you go inside the room?

B1   Just a small room, rather dark, one
          window and the shutters

SALTER   not very tidy I expect

B1   that's right, not tidy the bed not made,
          couple of books, bag on the floor with
          clothes half out of it

SALTER   did he scream?

B1   and you know what he's like, not tidy,
          am I tidy you don't know do you but
          you'd guess not wouldn't you but you'd
          be wrong there because I'm meticulous.

SALTER   What I want to know is how you
          actually, what you, how you got him to
          go off to some remote because that's
          what I'm imagining, you don't shoot the
          lodger without the landlady hearing, I
          don't know if you did shoot I don't know
          why I say shoot you could have had a
          knife you could have strangled, I can't
          think he would have gone off with you
          because he was frightened which is why

but perhaps you talked you made him
feel or did you follow him or lie in wait
in some dark? and I don't know how
you found him there did you follow him
from his house when he left or follow
him from here last time he?

B1	I didn't need to tell you it had happened
SALTER	but you did so naturally I want to
B1	and I'm wishing I hadn't
SALTER	no I'm glad
B1	and I'm not telling you
SALTER	because I won't tell anyone
B1	and there's nothing more to be said.

SALTER   What about the others? or is he the only
one you hated because I loved him, I
don't love the others, you and I have got
common cause against the others don't
forget, I'm still hoping we'll make our
fortunes there. I'm going to talk to a
solicitor, I've been too busy not busy but
it's been like a storm going on I don't
know what's gone on, it's not been very
long ago it all started. You're not going
to be a serial, wipe them all out so
you're the only, back like it was at the
start I'd understand that. If they do
catch up with you, I'm sure they won't
I'm sure you know what you're, if they
do we'll tell them it was me it was my
fault anyway you look at it. Don't you

agree, don't you feel that? Don't stop
talking to me. It wasn't his fault, you
should have killed me, it's my fault you.
Perhaps you're going to kill me, is that
why you've stopped talking? Shall I kill
myself? I'd do that for you if you like,
would you like that?

I'll tell you a thought, I could have killed
you and I didn't. I may have done
terrible things but I didn't kill you. I
could have killed you and had another
son, made one the same like I did or
start again have a different one get
married again and I didn't, I spared you
though you were this disgusting thing by
then anyone in their right mind would
have squashed you but I remembered
what you'd been like at the beginning
and I spared you, I didn't want a
different one, I wanted that again
because you were perfect just like that
and I loved you.

You know you asked me when you used
to shout in the night. Sometimes I was
there, I'd sit and listen to you or I'd not
be in any condition to hear you I'd just
be sitting. Sometimes I'd go out and
leave you. I don't think you got out
of bed, did you get out of bed, because
you'd be frightened what I'd do to you
so it was all right to go out. That was
just a short period you used to shout,
you grew out of that, you got so you'd

rather not see me, you wanted to be left alone in the night, you wouldn't want me to come any more. You'd nearly stopped speaking do you remember that? not speaking not eating I tried to make you. I'd put you in the cupboard do you remember? or I'd look for you everywhere and I'd think you'd got away and I'd find you under the bed. You liked it there I'd put your dinner under for you. But it got worse do you remember? There was nobody but us. One day I cleaned you up and said take him into care. You didn't look too bad and they took you away. My darling. Do you remember that? Do you remember that day because I don't remember it you know. The whole thing is very vague to me. It's two years I remember almost nothing about but you must remember things and when you're that age two years is much longer, it wasn't very long to me, it was one long night out. Can you tell me anything you remember? the day you left? can you tell me things I did I might have forgotten?

B1   When I was following him there was a time I was getting on the same train and he looked round, I thought he was looking right at me but he didn't see me. I got on the train and went with him all the way.

SALTER   Yes? yes?

5

SALTER *and* MICHAEL BLACK, *his son, thirty-five.*

MICHAEL   Have you met the others?

SALTER   You're the first.

MICHAEL   Are you going to meet us all?

SALTER   I thought I'd start.

MICHAEL   I'm sure everyone will be pleased to
            meet you. I know I am.

SALTER   I'm sorry to stare.

MICHAEL   No, please, I can see it must be. Do I
            look like?

SALTER   Yes of course

MICHAEL   of course, I meant

SALTER   no no I didn't mean

MICHAEL   I suppose I meant how

SALTER   because of course you don't, you don't,
            not exactly

MICHAEL   no of course

SALTER   I wouldn't mistake

MICHAEL   no

SALTER   or I might at a casual

MICHAEL   of course

SALTER   but not if I really look

MICHAEL   no

SALTER   no

MICHAEL   because?

SALTER   because of the eyes. You don't look at me in the same way.

MICHAEL   I'm looking at someone I don't know of course.

SALTER   Maybe you could tell me a little

MICHAEL   about myself

SALTER   if you don't mind

MICHAEL   no of course, it's where to, you already know I'm a teacher, mathematics, you know I'm married, three children did I tell you that

SALTER   yes but you didn't

MICHAEL   boy and girl twelve and eight and now a baby well eighteen months so she's walking and beginning to talk, I don't have any photographs on me I didn't think, there's no need for photographs is there if you see someone all the time so

SALTER   are you happy?

MICHAEL   what now? or in general? Yes I think I am, I don't think about it, I am. The

job gets me down sometimes. The
world's a mess of course. But you can't
help, a sunny morning, leaves turning,
off to the park with the baby, you can't
help feeling wonderful can you?

SALTER   Can't you?

MICHAEL   Well that's how I seem to be.

SALTER   Tell me. Forgive me

MICHAEL   no go on

SALTER   tell me something about yourself that's
really specific to you, something really
important

MICHAEL   what sort of?

SALTER   anything

MICHAEL   it's hard to

SALTER   yes.

MICHAEL   Well here's something I find fascinating,
there are these people who used to live
in holes in the ground, with all tunnels
and underground chambers and
sometimes you'd have a chamber you'd
get to it through a labyrinth of passages
and the ceiling got lower and lower so
you had to go on your hands and knees
and then wriggle on your stomach and
you'd get through to this chamber deep
deep down that had a hole like a
chimney like a well a hole all the way up
to the sky so you could sit in this

chamber this room this cave whatever
and look up at a little circle of sky going
past overhead. And when somebody died
they'd hollow out more little rooms so
they weren't buried underneath you they
were buried in the walls beside you. And
maybe sometimes they walled people up
alive in there, it's possible because of
how the remains were contorted but
either way of course they're dead by now
and very soon after they went in of
course. And

SALTER   I don't think this is what I'm looking for

MICHAEL   oh, how, sorry

SALTER   because what you're telling me is about
something else and I was hoping for
something about you

MICHAEL   I don't quite

SALTER   I'm sorry I don't know I was hoping

MICHAEL   you want what my beliefs, politics how
I feel about war for instance is that?
I dislike war, I'm not at all happy when
people say we're doing a lot of good
with our bombing, I'm never very
comfortable with that. War's one of those
things, don't you think, where everyone
always thinks they're in the right have
you noticed that? Nobody ever says
we're the bad guys, we're going to beat
shit out of the good guys. What do you
think?

SALTER   I was hoping I don't know something more personal something from deep inside your life. If that's not intrusive.

MICHAEL   Maybe what maybe my wife's ears?

SALTER   Yes?

MICHAEL   Because last night we were watching the news and I thought what beautiful and slightly odd ears she's got, they're small but with big lobes, big relative to the small ear, and they're slightly pointy on top, like a disney elf or little animal ears and they're always there but you know how you suddenly notice and noticing that, I mean the way I love her, felt very felt what you said something deep inside. Or the children obviously, I could talk about, is this the sort of thing?

SALTER   it's not quite

MICHAEL   no

SALTER   because you're just describing other people or

MICHAEL   yes

SALTER   not yourself

MICHAEL   but it's people I love so

SALTER   it's not what I'm looking for. Because anyone could feel

MICHAEL   oh of course I'm not claiming

SALTER   I was somehow hoping

MICHAEL   yes

SALTER   further in

MICHAEL   yes

SALTER   just about yourself

MICHAEL   myself

SALTER   yes

MICHAEL   like maybe I'm lying in bed and it's
              comfortable and then it gets slightly not
              so comfortable and I move my legs or
              even turn over and then it's

SALTER   no

MICHAEL   no

SALTER   no that's

MICHAEL   yes that's something everyone

SALTER   yes

MICHAEL   well I don't know. I like blue socks.
              Banana icecream. Does that help you?

SALTER   Dogs?

MICHAEL   do I like

SALTER   dogs

MICHAEL   I'm ok with dogs. My daughter wants a
              puppy but I don't know. Is dogs the kind
              of thing?

SALTER   So tell me what did you feel when you
            found out?

MICHAEL   Fascinated.

SALTER   Not angry?

MICHAEL   No.

SALTER   Not frightened.

MICHAEL   No, what of?

SALTER   Your life, losing your life.

MICHAEL   I've still got my life.

SALTER   But there are things there are things that
            are what you are, I think you're avoiding

MICHAEL   yes perhaps

SALTER   because then you might be frightened

MICHAEL   I don't think

SALTER   or angry

MICHAEL   not really

SALTER   because what does it do what does it to
            you to everything if there are all these
            walking around, what it does to me what
            am I and it's not even me it happened
            to, so how you can just, you must think
            something about it.

MICHAEL   I think it's funny, I think it's delightful

SALTER   delightful?

MICHAEL   all these very similar people doing things like each other or a bit different or whatever we're doing, what a thrill for the mad old professor if he'd lived to see it, I do see the joy of it. I know you're not at all happy.

SALTER   I didn't feel I'd lost him when I sent him away because I had the second chance. And when the second one my son the second son was murdered it wasn't so bad as you'd think because it seemed fair. I was back with the first one.

MICHAEL   But now

SALTER   now he's killed himself

MICHAEL   now you feel

SALTER   now I've lost him, I've lost

MICHAEL   yes

SALTER   now I can't put it right any more. Because the second time round you see I slept very lightly with the door open.

MICHAEL   Is that the worst you did, not go in the night?

SALTER   No of course not.

MICHAEL   Like what?

SALTER   Things that are what I did that are not trivial like banana icecream nor unifuckingversal like turning over in bed.

MICHAEL   We've got ninety-nine per cent the same
           genes as any other person. We've got
           ninety per cent the same as a chimpanzee.
           We've got thirty percent the same as a
           lettuce. Does that cheer you up at all?
           I love about the lettuce. It makes me feel
           I belong.

SALTER   I miss him so much. I miss them both.

MICHAEL   There's nineteen more of us.

SALTER   That's not the same.

MICHAEL   No of course not. I was making a joke.

SALTER   And you're happy you say are you? you
           like your life?

MICHAEL   I do yes, sorry.